ב"ה

לה' הארץ ומלואה

This book belongs to

_____

_____

_____

This book is dedicated to my parents who have full faith in me and encourage me to fulfil my dreams. May they continue to enjoy many more years in good health together.

Yisroel and the Pesach Salt Water
Part of the Jewish Discovery Series

First Edition - Shevat 5779 / January 2019
Copyright © 2019 by Amsy Books Limited
ALL RIGHTS RESERVED

ISBN: 978-1-9164311-0-2

Published by: Amsy Books Limited
Distributed in the UK by: Amsy Books Limited
info@amsybooks.com

Distributed in the USA/Canada & Israel by:
Ktav Publishers & Distributors Inc.
527 Empire Blvd. Brooklyn, NY 11225-3121
Tel: 718-972-5449, 201-963-9524
Fax: 718-972-6307, 201-963-0102
www.ktav.com

Also in The Jewish Discovery Series
Tova and the Shavuos Ice Pops
Yehuda and the Rain in the Succah

Printed in China

Jewish Discovery Series

Yisroel
and the
Pesach Salt Water

By Chaviva Pink
Illustrated by Shoshy Piltz

Today is
Erev Pesach.

Tonight we will
have a Seder.

Everyone is
helping to prepare
for Yom Tov.

Yisroel watches Shmuli peel the potatoes.

Yisroel watches Leah cut the apples.

Yisroel watches Tatty grate the marror.

Yisroel watches Mommy prepare the chicken soup.

Yisroel also wants to help.

"Mommy, can I help you get ready for Pesach?" he asks.

"Of course Yisroel," replies Mommy, "I have a special job that I am saving just for you."

He waits patiently until Mommy has finished putting the soup ingredients into the pot.

"Now it's your turn to help," says Mommy. "We are going to make **salt water**."

Yisroel remembers learning about salt water.

"Is salt water to remind us about the tears that the B'nei Yisroel cried in Mitzrayim?" he asks.

"That's right," says Mommy, giving him a big hug.

"Now let's begin. What ingredients do we need to make salt water?" asks Mommy.

Yisroel thinks. "Um, salt and water?" he answers.

"That's right," says Mommy.

Yisroel goes to get the salt. He puts it onto the kitchen table.

Mommy goes to get a jug of water, an empty bowl and two spoons. She puts them onto the kitchen table.

Mommy helps Yisroel to measure out
three spoons of salt, 1 - 2 - 3.

They put the salt into the empty bowl.

Then Mommy and Yisroel slowly add the water.
Yisroel can see the salt at the bottom of the bowl.

Yisroel takes the spoon and
starts to stir gently so that the
water does not splash.

Round and round the water goes. Yisroel stops stirring. He watches the water spinning around in the bowl. The water spins slower and slower until it stops moving.

Yisroel looks carefully into the water but cannot see the salt. Yisroel is surprised.

"Where has all the salt gone?" he asks.

"That is a very good question!" says Mommy. "The salt is still in the water. You cannot see it because it has **dissolved**. This means that the little bits of salt have broken up into even smaller pieces and have mixed with the water.

The salt has not disappeared. We know this because if you taste the water, it is salty."

Yisroel dipped his finger into the salt water and licked it. "Oo!" he shrieked as he scrunched up his face, "it tastes so salty."

Tatty, Shmuli and Leah come over to the table to see what Yisroel is getting so excited about.

"What is that? Is that a special type of Pesach drink? Shmuli asks.

"No, this is salt water" answers Yisroel proudly.

"I can't see any salt." says Leah.

Yisroel explains how the salt has **dissolved** into the water to make salt water.

"Hey, this reminds me about something else." says Tatty. "We know He is there but we just can't see Him. Does anyone know to Whom I am referring?" asks Tatty.

"Hashem, of course," answer all the children. Tatty smiles.

Mommy looks at her watch. "Wow, it's late. Time for our Erev Pesach rest." Mommy covers the salt water.

As Yisroel passes the table on his way to his room, he whispers to the salt water,

"See you later, at the Seder."

Glossary

Erev - Eve of

Pesach - Passover

Seder - Festival service/meal on the first two nights of Pesach

Yom Tov - Jewish festival

Marror - Bitter herbs

B'nei Yisroel - Jewish people

Mitzrayim - Egypt

Hashem - G-d

Experiment Activity

We want to find out:
Which substances can *dissolve* in water?

You will need:
4 glasses of water
1 teaspoon of sugar
1 teaspoon of salt
1 teaspoon of sand
1 teaspoon of rice

Instructions:

1) Fill all the glasses with the same amount of water.

2) Put 1 teaspoon of sugar into the first glass.

3) Stir it for 30 seconds.

4) Watch what happens to the sugar.

5) Now do the same with the salt, sand and rice. Put each one into a different glass. Stir each glass one at a time and watch what happens.

6) What are your observations? (What can you see happening?)

Results:

· When you put the sugar in the water and stir, it **dissolves**.

· When you put the salt in the water and stir, it **dissolves**.

· The sugar and salt are **soluble**.

· When you put the rice in the water and stir, it does not **dissolve**.

· When you put the sand in the water and stir, it does not **dissolve**.

· The rice and sand are not **soluble**.

Extra Activity:

Try adding a teaspoon of oil into a new glass of water.

What observations can you make?

Is oil **soluble** in water?

Now think of other substances that you can mix with water.

Observe what happens.

Which other substances are **soluble** in water?

Have fun discovering the wonders of the fascinating
world that Hashem has made for us.
Now get ready to find out:
How does water freeze? Where does rain come from?
In the next books of the **Jewish Discovery Series**.

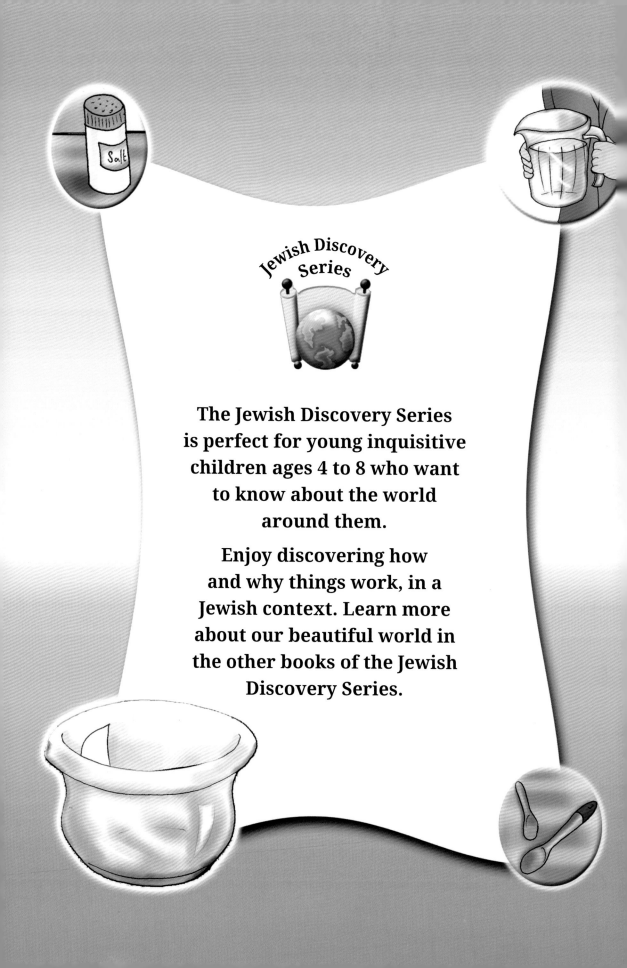

Jewish Discovery Series

The Jewish Discovery Series is perfect for young inquisitive children ages 4 to 8 who want to know about the world around them.

Enjoy discovering how and why things work, in a Jewish context. Learn more about our beautiful world in the other books of the Jewish Discovery Series.